Trail Mix of Thoughts

Blend of Ideas, Poems & Life

Kaavya Rajiv

BookLeaf Publishing
India | USA | UK

Made with ❤ on the BookLeaf Publishing Platform
www.bookleafpub.in
www.bookleafpub.com

In loving memory of my Grandfather & Bua

who taught me

my way with words.

Acknowledgement

This collection would not have come to life without the support and encouragement of many remarkable individuals.

First, I am deeply grateful to my grandmother & my parents, whose belief in the power of words shaped my own, and to my cousins, who have always been my sounding board and source of inspiration. Your unwavering support means the world to me.

A heartfelt thanks to my publisher, BookLeaf Publishing, for their keen eye and thoughtful guidance. Their expertise and insight have helped refine these poems into what they are today.

To my fellow poets and friends, for their constant inspiration, honest feedback, and the community we've created around our shared love of poetry. You've made the writing journey not only possible but truly meaningful.

I also wish to thank the readers—those who take a moment to pause and engage with these words. It is your connection to the poems that transforms them from mere ink on a page into something living and breathing.

Lastly, I dedicate this book to my late Grandfather & late Bua, whose spiritual influence has been a constant thread throughout my work. Your heavenly blessings are woven into every line.

Thank you all for your encouragement and for believing in the power of poetry to touch the soul.

With deep gratitude,

Kaavya Rajiv

Preface

This collection of poems is an exploration of thought, a trail of words that meander through the landscapes of the mind—sometimes winding and unsure, other times sharp and definitive. It is an invitation to walk with me, in no particular order, through the chaos and calm of internal dialogue. Each poem here is a fragment, a moment plucked from the whole, yet somehow, together, they form a larger tapestry of experience.

I did not set out with a clear map, nor did I know exactly where these words would lead. These poems are as much a surprise to me as they may be to you. They are reflections of thoughts half-formed and fully realized, of questions asked and some left unanswered. At times they linger in uncertainty, other times they seek resolution, but always, they pulse with the same thread of curiosity and the desire to understand.

What you will find here is not a neat narrative or a linear progression, but rather a collection of trails—some straight, some winding, some looping back on themselves—that speak to the fragmented nature of thought itself. The mind, like the poem, does not follow a straight line. It is fluid, restless, often contradictory, and endlessly fascinating.

This book is for anyone who has ever found themselves lost in thought, wondering how the seemingly disconnected parts of the world and the self can ever make sense. It is for those who find beauty in the broken, in the in-between moments, and in the rawness of unpolished thoughts. Above all, it is for anyone willing to let go of certainty and walk alongside these words, wherever they may lead.

Welcome to the journey.

Kaavya Rajiv

Celebration

That brings us together,
Makes our stories known,
It ignites the fire of love,
That all bonds are forged in,
A trial by flame,
Its depth, untold.
That brings a smile to our faces,
and warmth to our hearts,
And for a while,
our worries are gone,
They are just us, all together
Our strength is in numbers
And value in each other,
That is what celebration truly is.

Limit

The end for many,
The start for some,
Limits are borders,
And borders,
Are meant to be crossed,
Crush your limits,
Then you'll fly,
No one can stop you,
You have no limits,
Destroy your fear,
Apprehension, don't hold dear.
You can do it,
Don't listen to what others say,
If you do, do it to prove them wrong,
Even the sky isn't your limit,
The world is yours.

This poem is dedicated to all those whom the world underestimates.

Zoo

A zoo
A place where:
Wings meant to fly,
Are captive,
In cages,
A place where lives are on display,
Showpieces for us to see,
When no one understands...
That they matter too,
We are no different,
From them,
We have lives,
So do they,
We yearn for freedom,
And they do too,
So when will we realise
That it's wrong to lock them up?
When will humans learn about humanity?
Oh, when.....?

The Deeps and Shallows

The sea, vast and wild
How small it makes me feel!
Full of depths, undiscovered
Its magnificence has me enthralled
My gaze is frozen, I watch in glee
Unknown yet so beautiful
The sea is a poet's dream!

Beyond the horizon

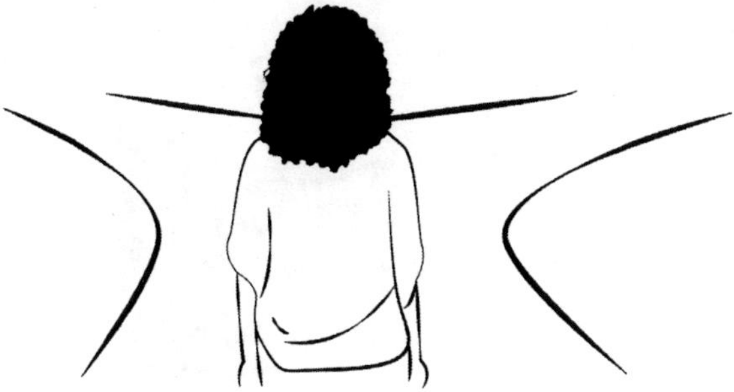

Beyond the horizon
What lies there?
The unknown,
Invites, to discover,
Within.
Overlook,
Or if you dare,
Venture,
Beyond the horizon,
Where the world we know ends,
Where risk takes the lead,
But discoveries are wonderful,
The unknown holds many things,
It's yet to say,
So be the first to listen to its stories,
One fine day.

Waterfalls

Waterfalls,
A show of might,
Power and strength,
Grace and danger at once,
A clash of qualities,
The raging stream of water,
That transforms into a gentle flow,
An imposing structure,
Pure creation,
This is what beauty is in its truest form,
We just cannot comprehend...
What it's capable of,
A commanding presence,
The aura surrounding it...
Is one of dominance and danger,
One of nature's most stunning displays.

Fireflies

Fireflies...
In the dark so empty
And so very bleak
They blink and twinkle
Like little stars
On the trees, not quite as far
A moment that can't be captured.
As mesmerising as the stars in the sky,
Perhaps even better, they shine.
Their brief moments of light,
Reminders of our short existence.
For now, Eden is here
This is paradise
One that will never be forgotten.

Trees

The silent denizens of the field and forest
From the mountain to the desert,
The protectors of the world
The keepers of the secrets of Earth
The ones who watch on,
They have seen it all.
They know it all.
Their wisdom is unmatched,
They give the breath of life,
They deserve respect.

The Sea

Until I saw the sea
I used to be someone different,
Until I saw the sea, the breeze,
Everything everyone could be,
I saw the light,
When I opened my eyes,
One day,
And everything I used to believe...
Was gone,
I became a new person,
When I saw the sea,
And realised,
That there was more to life than I thought,
The sea woke me up,
Everyone has a "Sea"
That they'll one day experience,
Maybe now,
Or maybe later.

The sound of Silence

The sound of silence
Louder than music,
Screams or arguments,
The honking of horns,
They all stop eventually,
But the sound of silence,
Can quiet them all,
A silence so loud,
It deafens,
Silence can change everything,
Thoughts turn around
The world can stop,
When you stop the sound.

Poem

An expression of the soul,
More than just words,
Not just descriptions,
But ways to look at the world—
Perceptions, they are
Different for each of us,
Unique pieces of knowledge,
Beauty that unfolds,
Like a lotus in the water,
Clean despite the mud,
They are our means,
To see clearly and truly,
Poems are deep,
They are not just eloquence,

They are much more,
They are a reflection of who we are.
An ethereal mirror,
Yet, here I ask:
What are they….to you?

Happiness

Living, Loving, and Lying,
Getting caught in the crowd,
Money, fame, and pleasure,
We forget all else,
In the end, we recall
What had truly mattered,
No one regrets happiness,
For it's what floats your boat,
Happiness is divine,
We just cannot comprehend,
Nevertheless, I ask you this:
What is happiness?

Breeze

Oh, the breeze
Gentle and Serene,
Forever changing speed
Making the trees sway
Making the flowers fall
Ever present, always different
Sometimes hot, sometimes cold
Sometimes calm, sometimes not
Never will it be the same
Its unpredictability is its beauty
Its wildness is its Grace.

Autumn leaves and Lost memories

Oh, the leaves,
The lost memories,
That rustle as we walk over them,
Yet we don't recall...
Them,
As they fall,
Like leaves from a tree,
In autumn,
As the moonlight makes way...
For a new dawn,
A new day,
When the autumn leaves fall,

And the memories fade,
When it all falls apart,
To create a new picture,
A whole new world,
Wonderous,
Like before,
Only to shatter again.
So raise your eyes,
Respect what is no more,
Maybe they'll be back
One day,
One fine autumn day...

Memories

Memories, Forgotten or Remembered
They are always there,
Sometimes resurfacing,
Like ripples across the water,
A memory is a moment that is gone.
Like a picture, forever to remain,
Etched in the mind,
Memories are precious,
We must hold them close,
They hold more value than diamonds and
gold,
Keep the memories,
Never let go.

The Meadow

A meadow,
However small,
Is a vast and unending space—
Not in length,
But in detail
Every blade of grass
Every twig on the tree
Is a world in which
Thousands of tales can be told,
A fairytale land,
Right under our eyes.
Ever better,
Than the ones in books.

Invisible threads

The threads
That hold the world together,
That weave our homes,
They are stronger than mere string,
They are threads of memories,
Of feelings,
Of hopes, dreams, and truth,
Of wonder and peace,
They remain unseen,
But they hold us all,
And they form the world,
And the thoughts
Of us all.

Ocean

The deep waters,
Deeper than just the trench,
It goes down,
The oceanic silence,
The feeling of solitude,
The calm that pervades,
The senses,
The rooted sensation of wonder,
Reaches a new height,
A beautiful world,
Better to see,
Alone,
Away from the human world,
Into the new one,
This is the real calm.

Beneath the Cracks

A whole new world,
One entirely unnoticed,
Yet it's there,
Beneath the cracks,
The wonder unfolds,
If you take the time to notice,
What is usually overlooked,
You'll see the world,
All of it,
You'll see the ones,
We don't notice,
That's the beauty in all,
It is a charm,
A treat for sore eyes,

If you ever see it,
You'll know what I mean,
Beauty and pain in one.

Starlight Fades

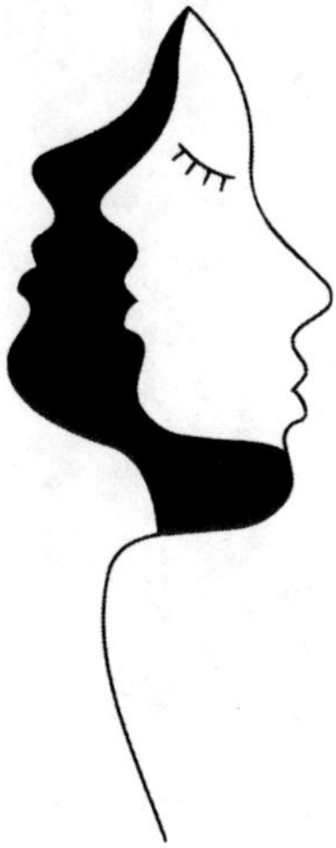

Starlight Fades
So does the moon,
Everything alive,
Gone so soon?
It's a harsh truth,
That everything wanes,
It feels too early,
Much too soon,
No time to say goodbye,
Why, we ask.
Hating the force
That grinds all to a halt,
But everything has to end,

That's the beauty of beginning,
What is end,
But a time to rest,
After a long, weary day?

Whispers of the wind

Dreams that never came to be,
Moments that were lost,
Memories that were forgotten,
And those who couldn't find their paths,
This is their cry, one of pain,
Of sorrow untold,
Their stories remain forgotten,
Never to be recalled,
Oh, listen,
To what they say,
They have lived too,
Even forgotten, they live on,
In the whispers of the wind.